Yes You Can,
Little Brown Boy

Written By: Alicia Washington

Illustrated By: Ny'Shawn Johnson & Alicia Washington

This story is dedicated to my two sons, Dexter Caleb and Jeremiah Reid, and all the boys and girls that need a little encouragement overcoming milestones!

Love Always,

Alicia <3

Hello! This is Aaron and his favorite word is CAN'T. After today, he will know he CAN do anything his heart desires as long as he believes in himself.

"I can't pull up my pants! It's too hard," said Aaron as he frowned with defeat. "Yes You Can, Little Brown Boy. Take your time and do one leg at a time," said his Mommy.

Aaron took a deep breath, got both legs in and pulled up his pants. He smiled with excitement!

"I can't put on my shirt! My head is stuck!" said Aaron as he removes his shirt and throws it. "Yes You Can, Little Brown Boy. Hold the opening on each side and pull down," said his Daddy.

Aaron took a deep breath, held his shirt over his head, pulled it down and brought his arms through! "I did it!" He yelled with excitement.

"I can't tie my shoes!" yelled Aaron as he stomps in place. "Yes You Can, Little Brown Boy. Say the steps as you tie," said his Mommy.

Aaron took a deep breath and said the steps out loud. "Make two loops, wrap one around. Pull the loop through and you've tied your shoe!" He dabbed with excitement when he succeeded.

While writing his name, Aaron had trouble with the letter A. "I'll never be able to write my name," he yelled. "Yes You Can, Little Brown Boy. Remember the rhyme and you will get it every time," said his Daddy.

Aaron took a deep breath and sung the rhyme. "Up, Down, Across. I'm making A's like a Boss! I did it! I did it!" He yelled and kept practicing.

Aaron was riding his tricycle, but kept pedaling backwards instead of forward. He yelled out, "I can't go forward!" "Yes You Can, Little Brown Boy. Sing the tune Mommy taught you," said his Mommy.

Aaron took a deep breath and sung the song as he pedaled along. "Push to the right, push to the left. I'm riding my tricycle because I tried my best," he sung and was riding like a pro in no time!

Once Aaron stopped saying CAN'T, he realized he could do anything he put his mind to.

I CAN!!!

YES YOU CAN, LITTLE BROWN BOY!

THE
END